D0569001

Bastien Piano Basics

THEORY

LEVEL 3

BY JAMES BASTIEN

Contents

*To reinforce the feeling of achievement, the teacher or student may put a √ when the page has been completed.

ISBN 0-8497-5275-2

© **1985 Neil A. Kjos Music Company**, 4380 Jutland Drive, San Diego, California 92117.
International copyright secured. All rights reserved. Printed in U.S.A.
Warning! The contents of this publication are protected by copyright law. To copy or reproduce
them by any method is an infringement of the copyright law. Anyone who reproduces copyrighted matter
is subject to substantial penalties and assessments for each infringement.

2

Boogie Bass

Many different accompaniment styles can be used to harmonize melodies.
The **boogie bass** uses the first, fifth, and sixth tones of the scale.

Scale tones: 1   5   6   5

1. Write the boogie bass for measures 2-5. Play as written, then transpose to C and F.

Key of _____

5   2   1

2. Write the boogie bass for measures 2-7, then play this piece.

Express Train Boogie

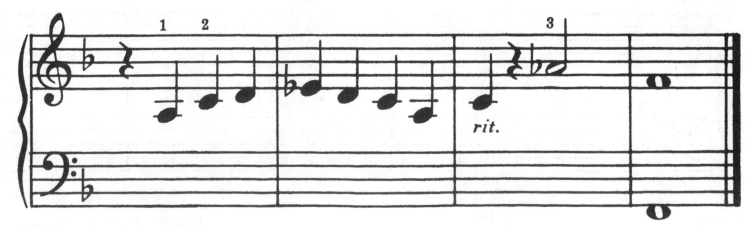

Writing Major Sharp Key Signatures

The **order of sharps** is F C G D A E B.

To write a key signature for a specific sharp key, draw the sharps in their order until you draw the sharp before the keynote.

Key of D Major

Keynote

Sharp **before** the keynote

3. Draw these Major key signatures.

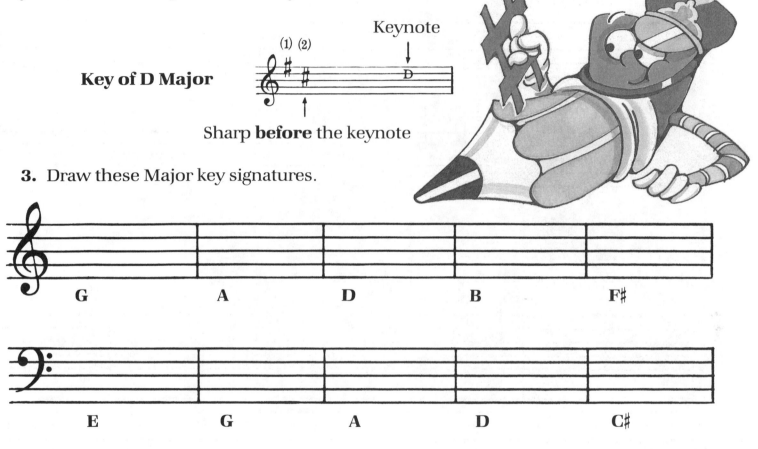

G   A   D   B   F♯

E   G   A   D   C♯

4. Draw these Major key signatures in both clefs.

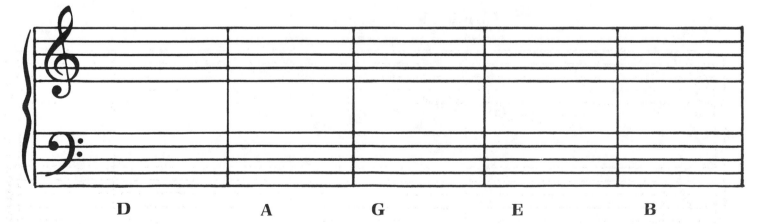

D   A   G   E   B

A Minor Scale (Relative to C Major)

Relative Major and minor scales have the **same** key signature.
The relative minor scale begins on the **6th** tone of the Major scale.

There are three forms of minor scales: **natural, harmonic, melodic**.

5. Draw the notes of the A **natural** minor scale.
   Use the same tones as the relative Major scale.

C Major Scale

A Natural Minor Scale

6. Draw the notes of the A **harmonic** minor scale.
   Raise the 7th tone one half step.

Up   Down

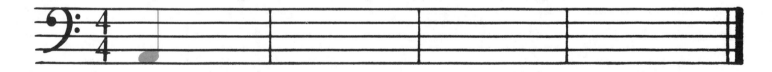

7. Draw the notes of the A **melodic** minor scale.
   Raise the 6th and 7th tones going up; lower them coming down.

Up   Down

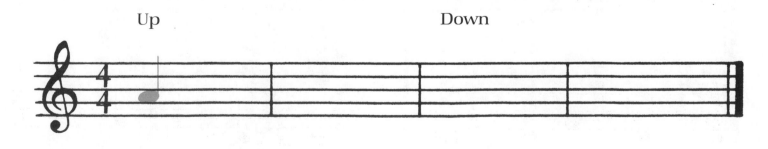

Minor Key Signatures

The **same** key signature is used for relative Major and minor keys.
You can find the minor key by counting down **three half steps** from the Major key.

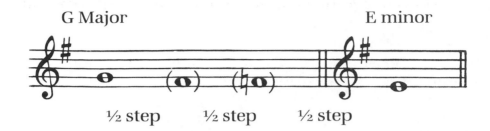

½ step   ½ step   ½ step

8. Write the names of the minor keys on the blank lines.

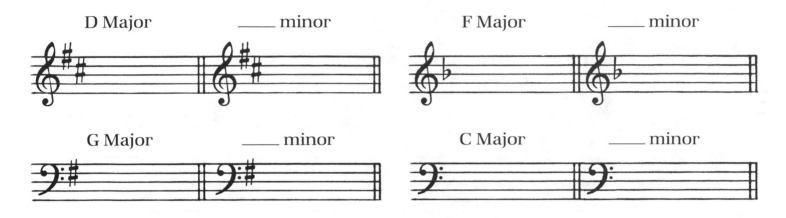

9. To tell whether a piece is in Major or minor, look at the first and last notes.
Play each melody below and listen to the sound.
Write the names of the Major or minor keys on the blank lines.

Major and Minor Triads

The intervals in Major and minor triads are:

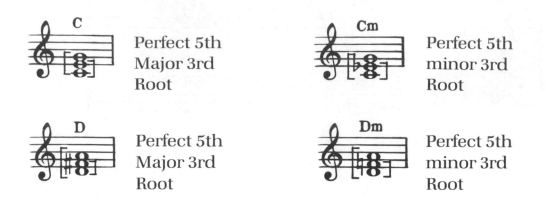

C
Perfect 5th
Major 3rd
Root

Cm
Perfect 5th
minor 3rd
Root

D
Perfect 5th
Major 3rd
Root

Dm
Perfect 5th
minor 3rd
Root

10. First, draw the Major triad. Next, draw the minor triad (lower the middle note one half step). Play these Major and minor chords.

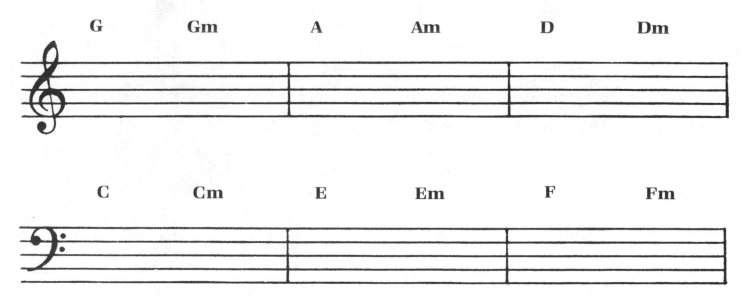

| G | Gm | A | Am | D | Dm |

| C | Cm | E | Em | F | Fm |

11. Write the names of these Major and minor triads, then play them.

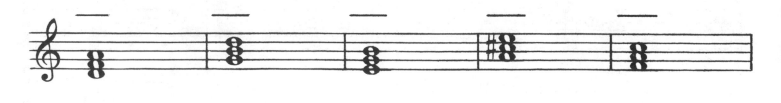

Primary Chords in A Minor

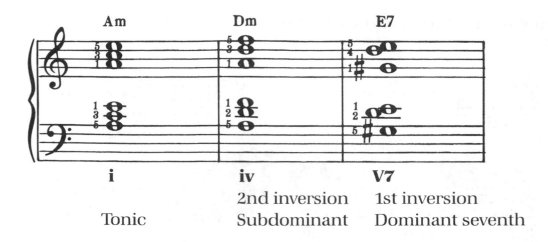

Am	Dm	E7
i	iv	V7
Tonic	2nd inversion Subdominant	1st inversion Dominant seventh

12. Draw the primary chords in A minor, then play them.

This sign means *alla breve* or "cut time."
There are two strong beats in each measure.

13. Draw the primary chords in
the bass clef, then play this piece.

Winter Wind

Use with pages 12-13 of Piano, Level 3. **WP208**

Broken Chord Bass (1st Style)

There are many kinds of **broken chord bass** patterns.
This one uses notes of a chord played one note at a time.

14. Write this broken chord bass for measures 2-7.
Play as written, then transpose to G, F, D, A, and E.

Circle Dance

Key of _____

Moderato

Question and Answer Phrases

15. Make up (improvise) two-measure answer phrases to complete these lines. Write your best answers on the staffs.

16. Write a melody and the harmony indicated by the chord symbols to complete these lines.

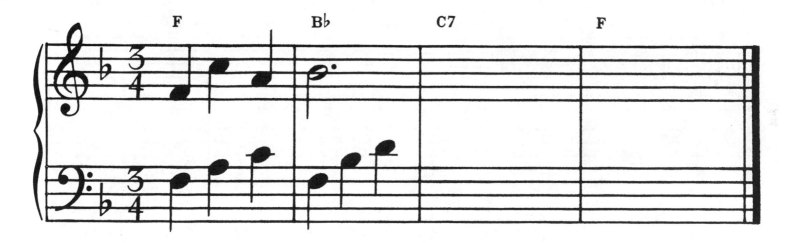

D Minor Scale (Relative to F Major)

17. Draw the notes of the D **natural** minor scale. Use the same tones as the relative Major scale.

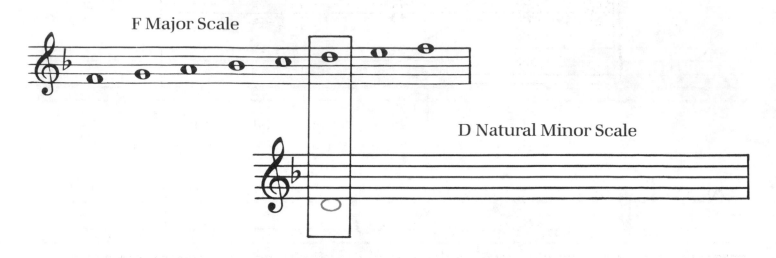

F Major Scale

D Natural Minor Scale

18. Draw the notes of the D **harmonic** minor scale in both clefs. Raise the 7th tone one half step.

Up   Down

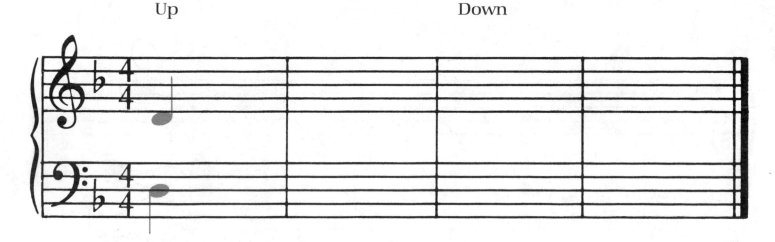

19. Draw the notes of the D **melodic** minor scale in both clefs. Raise the 6th and 7th tones going up; lower them coming down.

Up   Down

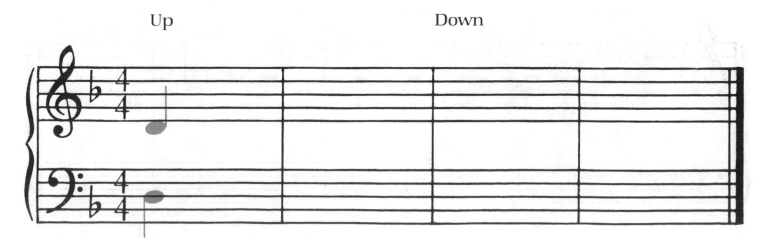

Primary Chords in D Minor

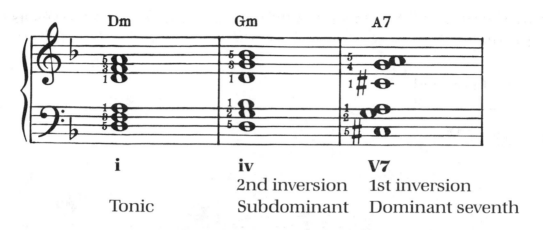

Dm	Gm	A7
i	**iv**	**V7**
	2nd inversion	1st inversion
Tonic	Subdominant	Dominant seventh

20. Draw the primary chords in D minor, then play them.

21. Draw the primary chords in the bass clef, then play this piece.

Storm at Sea

Allegro

Triads and Inversions

Any root position triad may be **inverted** (rearranged) by moving the root note to the **top** or **middle**. (*Note:* the root is the **top** note of the 4th in an inversion.)

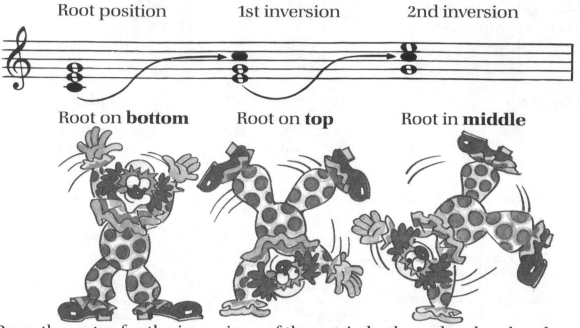

22. Draw the notes for the inversions of these triads, then play the chords.

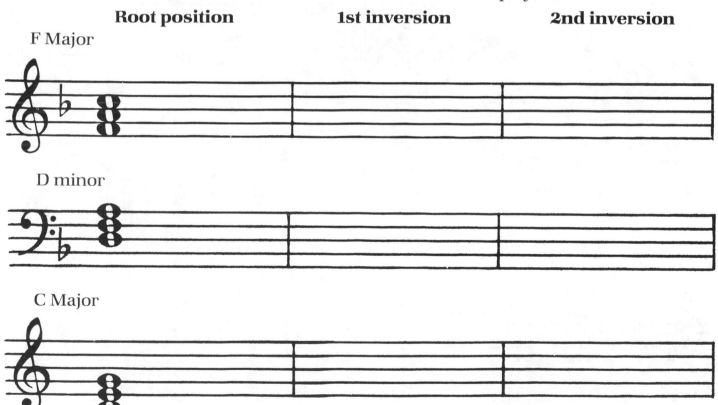

Root position   **1st inversion**   **2nd inversion**

F Major

D minor

C Major

A minor

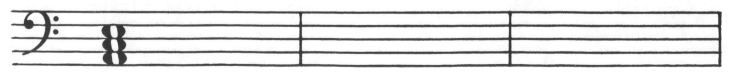

Recognizing Inverted Triads

1st inversion triads have two notes at
the bottom that are close together,
forming an interval of a 3rd.
The root is always the **top** note in the
interval of the 4th.

3rd [] 4th

23. Circle the root and write the name of each 1st inversion triad,
then play these chords.

F ___ ___ ___ ___ ___

___ ___ ___ ___ ___ ___

2nd inversion triads have two notes
at the top that are close together,
forming an interval of a 3rd.
The root is always the **top** note in the
interval of the 4th.

3rd [ ] 4th

24. Circle the root and write the name of each 2nd inversion triad,
then play these chords.

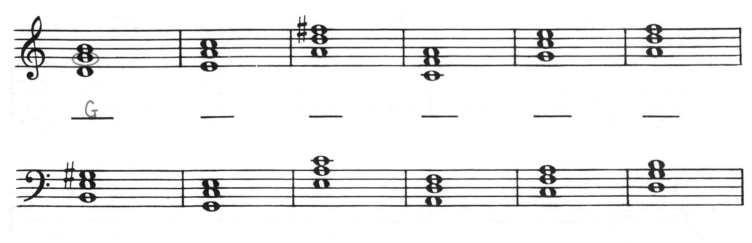

G ___ ___ ___ ___ ___

___ ___ ___ ___ ___ ___

14

Triplet Rhythm

A **triplet** figure is usually indicated by a **3** and a **slur** placed next to the beam.

A triplet eighth note figure is equal to one quarter note.

25. Draw a triplet note figure between each quarter note. Clap and count this rhythm.

26. Write a **3** and draw a slur for the triplet figures in measures 2-7, then play this piece.

Triplets

Moderato

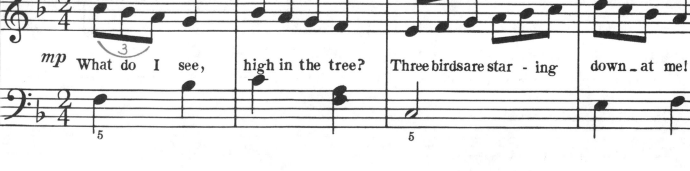

mp What do I see, high in the tree? Three birds are star - ing down _ at me!

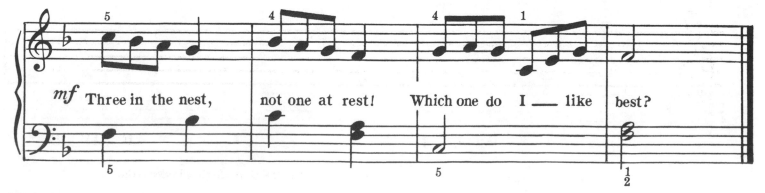

mf Three in the nest, not one at rest! Which one do I _ like best?

WP208 *Use with pages 22-23 of* Piano, Level 3.

Ledger Lines

The short lines above and below the staff are called **ledger lines**.
Ledger lines extend (stretch) the staff's range up or down.

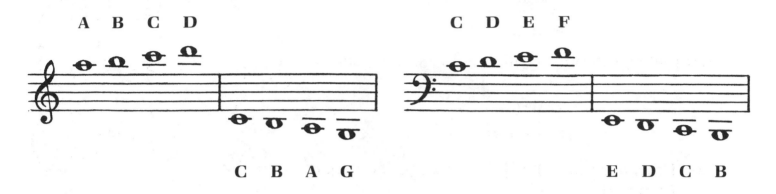

27. Write the names of these ledger line and space notes, then play them.

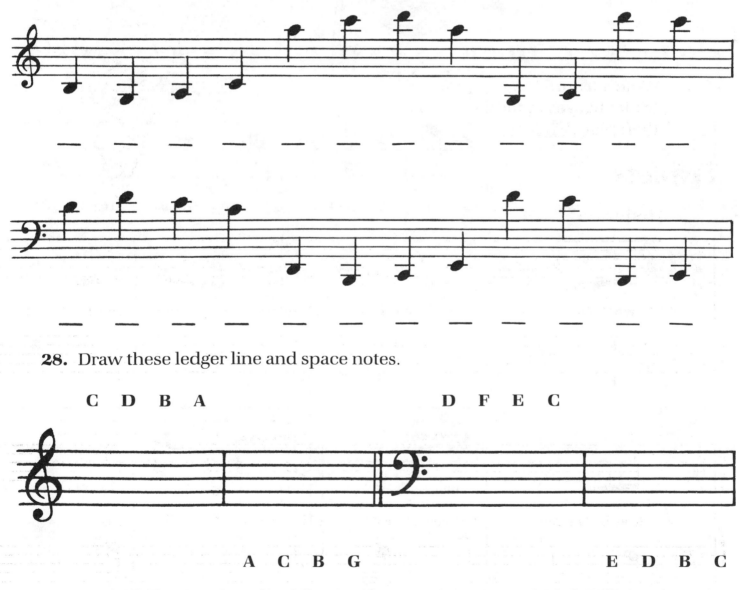

28. Draw these ledger line and space notes.

Teacher: Have the student drill on these notes using the **Bastien Music Flashcards.**

Use with pages 24-25 of Piano, Level 3. **WP208**

Broken Chord Bass (2nd Style)

29. Write this broken chord bass in the blank measures below. Play as written, then transpose to C, F, D, A, and E.

Home Sweet Home

Moderato

mp Through — man-sions and | pal - a - ces, | though — we may | roam, Be it

ev - er so | hum - ble, there's | no ___ place like | home!

8th (Octave)

An interval of an **8th**, called an **octave**, is either line to space or space to line.

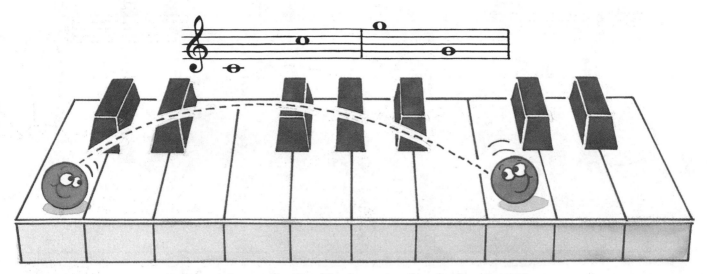

30. Write the names of these **melodic intervals**, then play them.

31. Draw a half note **after** the one written to form a melodic octave, then play each one.

32. Write the names of these **harmonic intervals**, then play them.

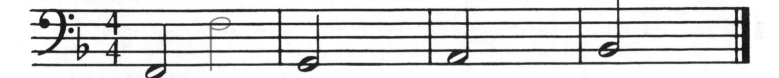

33. Draw a whole note **below** the one written to form a harmonic octave, then play each one.

Waltz Bass

34. Write the waltz bass in the bass clef. Play as written, then transpose to C, F, and G.

Black Cat Waltz

Allegretto

Alberti Bass

35. Write the Alberti bass in the bass clef. Play as written, then transpose to F, G, D, A, and E.

March!

Alla marcia

The Chromatic Scale

The **chromatic scale** is made of twelve half steps (one octave).
It may begin on **any** note.

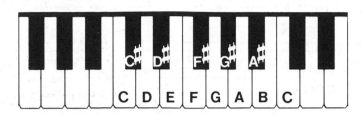

Fingering Pattern

Use 3 on the black keys.
Use 1 on the white keys, except when two white keys are together. Then use fingers 1-2 or 2-1.

36. Write the chromatic scale going **up**. Use sharps for the black keys. Write the fingering over the notes, then play what you have written.

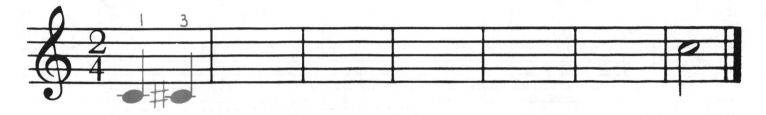

37. Write the chromatic scale going **down**. Use flats for the black keys. Write the fingering under the notes, then play what you have written.

38. Write the fingering for these chromatic scales, then play them.

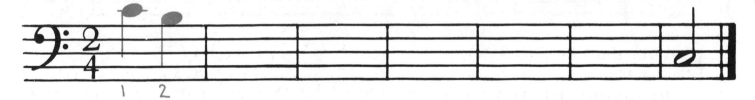

The Order of Flats

Memorize this order of flats!

39. Write the order of flats two times on each staff.

40. The order of flats is **B E A D G C F.**
The order of sharps is **F C G D A E B.**
Notice that the order of sharps is just the opposite of the order of flats!

Teacher: Have the student continue writing the order of flats in the **Bastien Music Notebook**.

Major Flat Key Signatures

To find the name of a Major **flat key**:

1. Name the **next-to-the-last** flat in the key signature.
2. The letter name of this flat is the name of the Major key, with the *exception* of F Major, which has only one flat.

41. Write the names of these Major flat key signatures.

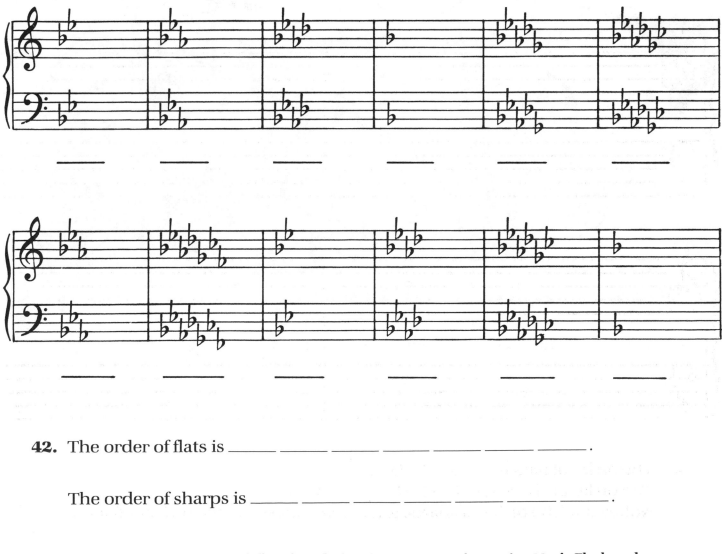

42. The order of flats is _____ _____ _____ _____ _____ _____ _____ .

The order of sharps is _____ _____ _____ _____ _____ _____ _____ .

Teacher: Have the student drill on these flat key signatures using the **Bastien Music Flashcards**.

Ledger Line Review

43. Write the names of these ledger line and space notes, then play them.

Minor Key Signature Review

44. Write the names of these minor key signatures. Refer to page 5 if necessary.

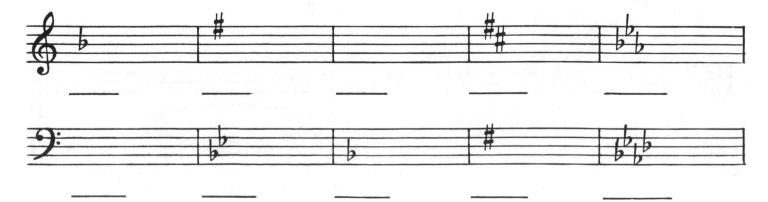

Group 3 Keys (D♭, A♭, E♭)

Each I chord in this group has a **white key** in the **middle**.

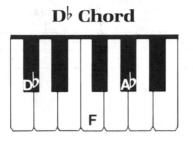
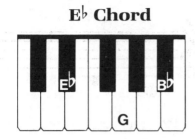

D♭ Chord   **A♭ Chord**   **E♭ Chord**

45. Draw whole notes to form these I chords, then play them.

D♭ Chord   A♭ Chord   E♭ Chord

46. Play these **solid** and **broken** chords in the Group 3 keys.

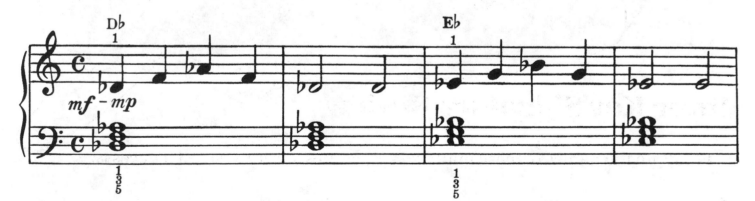

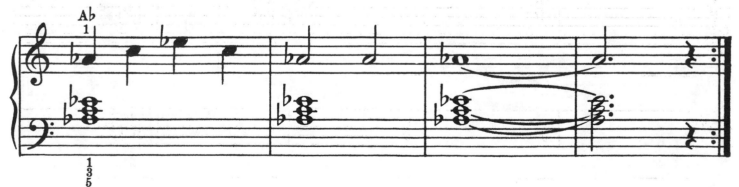

D♭ Major Scale

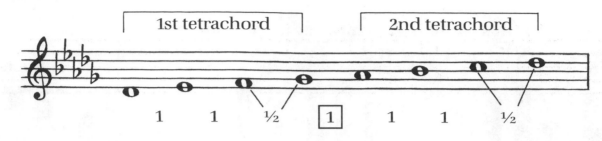

47. Draw the notes of the D♭ Major scale going **up**, then play them.

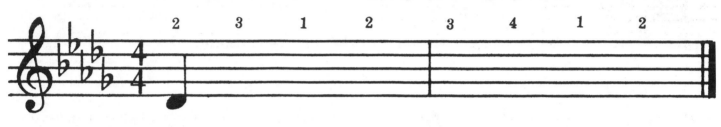

48. Draw the notes of the D♭ Major scale going **down**, then play them.

49. Write your own tempo and dynamics, then play this piece.

Spring Song

Primary Chords in D♭

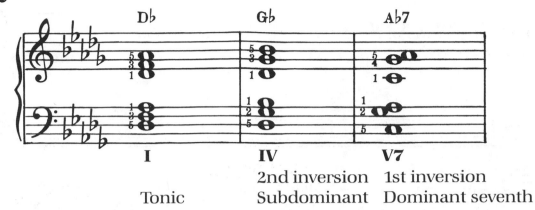

D♭	G♭	A♭7
I	IV	V7
Tonic	2nd inversion Subdominant	1st inversion Dominant seventh

50. Draw the primary chords in D♭ Major, then play them.

D♭   G♭   A♭7   D♭   G♭   A♭7

I   IV   V7   I   IV   V7

51. Draw the chords indicated. Write your own tempo and dynamics, then play this piece.

Michael, Row the Boat Ashore

Play this piece again using the **broken chord bass** (2nd style) shown on page 16.

Music Review Quiz

52. Draw these music signs.

First ending   Second ending

repeat sign   accent signs   natural signs

crescendo   diminuendo

53. What do these signs mean?

C _____   ¢ _____

54. What do these tempo marks mean?

allegro _____   andante _____

allegretto _____   moderato _____

55. Complete the following sentences.

ff means _fortissimo_ _____ or _very loud_ _____.

f means _____ or _____.

mf means _____ or _____.

p means _____ or _____.

pp means _____ or _____.

Score 10 points for each correct answer.
Perfect score: 180 points.

Your score: _____.

Triad and Inversion Review

56. Draw the notes for the inversions of these triads, then play these chords.

Root position   **1st inversion**   **2nd inversion**

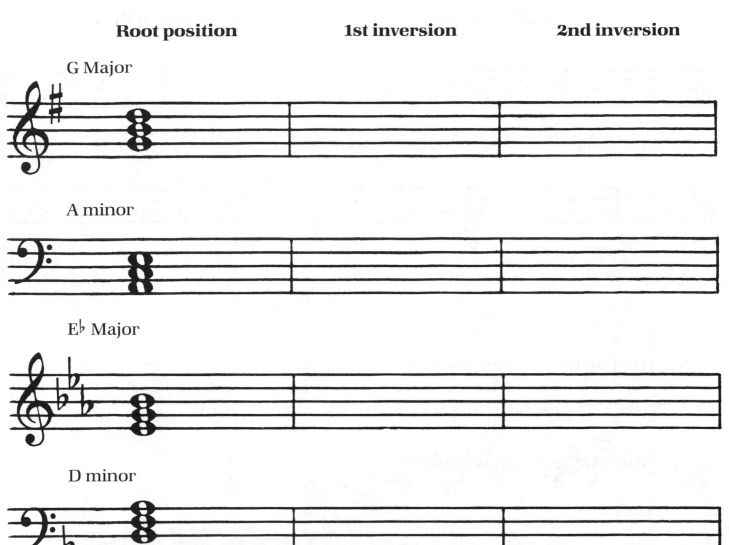

57. Circle the root and write the name of each 1st inversion triad,
then play these chords.

58. Circle the root and write the name of each 2nd inversion triad,
then play these chords.

A♭ Major Scale

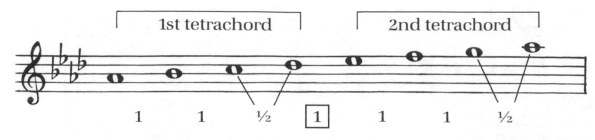

59. Draw the notes of the A♭ Major scale going **down**, then play them.

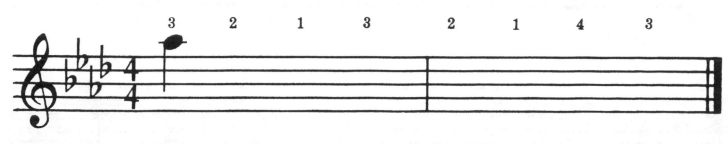

60. Draw the notes of the A♭ Major scale going **up**, then play them.

61. Write your own tempo and dynamics, then play this piece.

Winding River

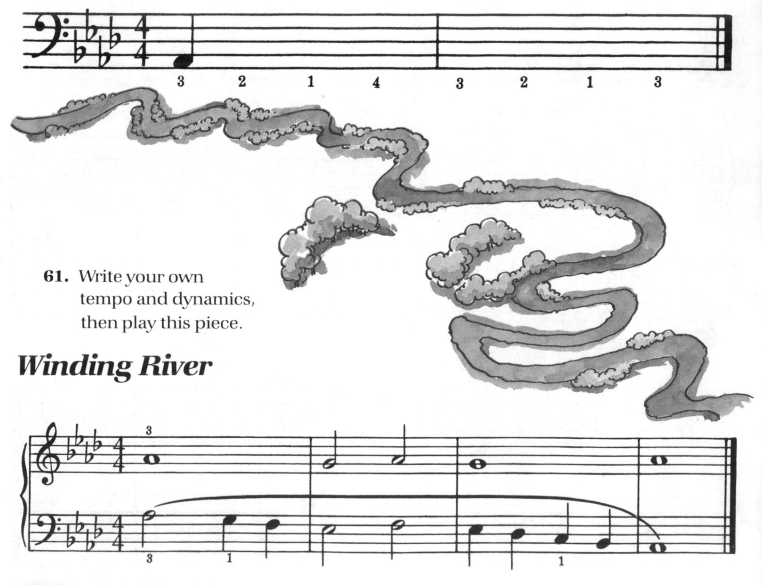

Primary Chords in A♭

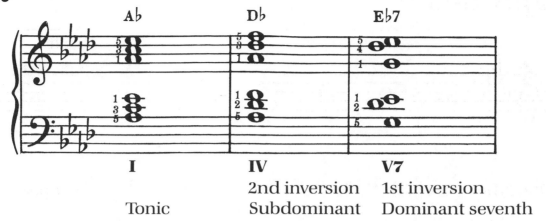

	2nd inversion	1st inversion
I	**IV**	**V7**
Tonic	Subdominant	Dominant seventh

62. Draw the primary chords in A♭ Major, then play them.

63. Draw the chords indicated. Write your own tempo and dynamics, then play this piece.

A Simple Gift

Shaker Song

Use with pages 46-47 of Piano, Level 3. **WP208**

E♭ Major Scale

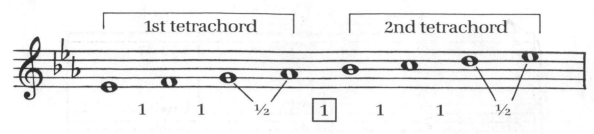

64. Draw the notes of the E♭ Major scale going **up**, then play them.

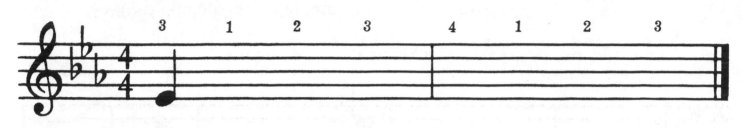

65. Draw the notes of the E♭ Major scale going **down**, then play them.

66. Write your own tempo and dynamics, then play this piece.

At the Beach

Primary Chords in E♭

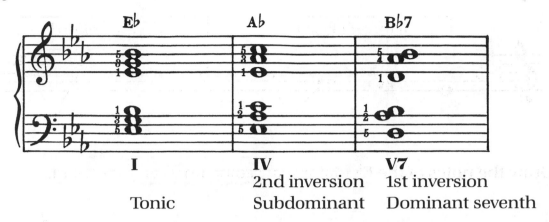

E♭	A♭	B♭7
I	IV	V7
	2nd inversion	1st inversion
Tonic	Subdominant	Dominant seventh

67. Draw the primary chords in E♭ Major, then play them.

E♭   A♭   B♭7   E♭   A♭   B♭7

I   IV   V7   I   IV   V7

68. Draw the chords indicated. Write your own tempo and dynamics, then play this piece.

Quick-Step Polka

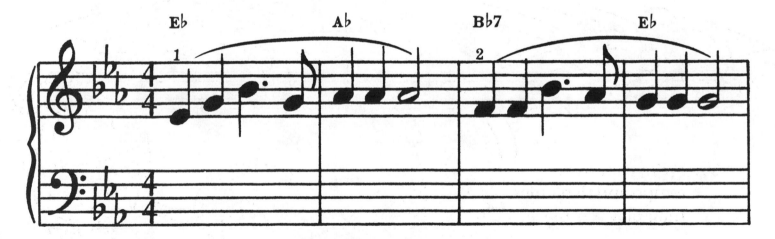

Music Review

69. Draw the order of sharps.

70. Draw the order of flats.

71. What is this rhythm called? _____

72. Write the names of these minor key signatures.

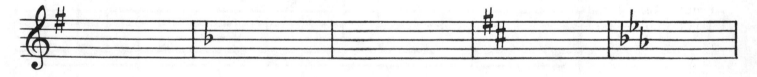

_____   _____   _____   _____   _____

73. Write the chromatic scale going up, starting on D.

74. The relative minor scale begins on the _____ tone of the Major scale.

75. Write the names of the three kinds of minor scales. _____

_____   _____